Tenors, Tantrums and Trills

An Opera Dictionary from Aida to Zzzz

Tenors, Tantrums and Trills

AN OPERA DICTIONARY FROM AIDA TO ZZZZ

David W. Barber

ILLUSTRATIONS BY
Dave Donald

SOUND AND VISION

DEDICATION

For my mother, Mollie Barber, for all her
encouragement and support, a long-overdue
gesture of gratitude.

Achilles

AUTHOR'S NOTE
AND ACKNOWLEDGEMENTS

I seem to be writing about opera a lot. Some sort of penance, I suppose. It could be worse: I could have to listen more and write less. Anyway, before anyone takes offence, let me hasten to say that most of the nasty things I say in this little dictionary I don't really mean. (Well, except maybe some of the stuff about Wagner.) And of course any resemblance to real persons living or dead is probably just a coincidence.

A note to the pedants: I know the subtitle of this book says "from Aida to Zzzz" and some of you will notice that Aida isn't actually the first entry. Well, come on. If I'd said "from Abandon to Zzzz," would that have been nearly as catchy?

The usual round of thanks to the usual people: To Geoff Savage of Sound And Vision for being a good and supportive publisher; to Dave Donald as always for his inspired illustrations; to my wife, Judy Scott, for her help with the manuscript and for putting up with me in its preparation. (Thanks to Brian Jackson for the *Can belto* joke.) And to you, the readers, for your kind letters and other words of encouragement over the years.

DWB
Westport and Toronto, 1996

A

Abandon: 1. A term to describe singing of a wild, uncontrolled nature, as often found in opera.
2. The best thing to do to singers performing in this manner.

Abduction: 1. A common operatic plot device (Mozart's *Abduction from the Seraglio*, Britten's *The Rape of Lucretia* and others) in which a singer is forcibly removed from the scene.
2. An event some operagoers think should happen more often — especially if kidnapping is the only way to get some really lousy singer off the stage.

Accent: 1. A musical or rhythmic stress, as on the first beat of a bar.
2. What many opera singers speak with.

Accidentals: Notes of pitches other than those indicated by the key signature. In other words, the polite term for mistakes, made by either the performer or composer.

Achilles: An ancient Greek hero, betrothed to Iphigenia (in Gluck's *Iphigenia in Aulis* and others). Unfaithful at first, he later rescues the heroine — proving he's not such a heel after all.

Addio: Italian for "goodbye." A term often found in operatic arias (*Addio alla madre*, from Mascagni's *Cavalleria Rusticana*; *Addio, fiorito asil*, Pinkerton's farewell from Puccini's *Madama Butterfly*; *O terra, addio*, from Verdi's *Aida* and so on). Sung at great length by performers before they actually leave. Sometimes this takes forever.

Ad libitum: From the Latin "at liberty," a style of music improvised or delivered freely, at the discretion of the performer. Often displayed by opera singers in cadenzas and the repeat sections of *Da Capo* arias. Not to be confused with "add Librium," a medicinal prescription often advisable (for conductors and other listeners) at such times.

Affections: 1. The feelings or emotions of music. In the late Baroque, these were codified into a doctrine of compositional technique.
2. Emotions often on display in opera productions, between principal singers, principals and chorus members and so on. Often likely to prove awkward and inconvenient when they sour.

Aida: A big, splashy opera by Giuseppi Verdi — you know, the one with the elephants. Commissioned in 1870 by the Khedive of Egypt to open the Suez Canal, *Aida* was not actually performed until a year after the party was over, thereby helping to maintain the long tradition of musicians never being ready on time.

Aida

Air: 1. An essential ingredient needed by singers in order to perform.
2. When hot, an ingredient found in great quantities in opera singers, who are full of it.
3. In the plural (airs), the kind of attitude many opera singers put on when before the public.

Alberich: A misshapen, ugly Nibelung dwarf, one of the central characters in Wagner's *Ring Cycle*. (In three of the four operas, anyway. He gets to sit out *Die Walküre*.) He later turns into a toad, which generally improves his looks.

Alto: A medium vocal range, lying between tenor and soprano. (A dangerous place to be.) Usually sung by women (see Contralto) but sometimes by men (see Counter-tenor).

Amen: A traditional expression of praise and thanksgiving found in closing scenes of some operas. Much more often to be heard from audience members grateful at finally being allowed to leave.

Ancora: An Italian term meaning "still" (*ancora forte*, still loud) or sometimes "again" (similar to *encore*). Not to be confused with *angora*, a type of wool much favored by opera singers for their sweaters.

Aria: A fancy, highfalutin Italian word that just means "song," used by opera types to try to impress other opera types (opera being essentially nothing more than a glorified form of oneupmanship anyway). The fact that people who sing such songs tend to be very large and swing out their arms a lot — that is, they take up a lot of area — is probably nothing more than an interesting linguistic coincidence.

Audience: 1. A formal meeting granted to one of lowly status in the presence of some exalted personage — as for instance (though rarely) with the Pope, or (even more rarely) with a famous opera singer.
2. The collection of people for whom — ostensibly, at least — an opera production is performed. Find a way to get rid of them and this whole opera problem might just go away.

B

Bach, J.S.: A German Baroque musician, considered by many to be the greatest composer who ever lived. He wrote no operas at all, which must have something to do with it.

Balance: 1. A state of musical equilibrium difficult but essential to attain among groups of singers and instrumentalists.
2. A state of mental equilibrium even more difficult but essential to attain among groups of singers and

J.S. Bach

instrumentalists, especially in opera.

Ballad opera: A type of light opera especially popular in 18th-century England (such as *The Beggar's Opera*) in which all the tunes are stolen from somewhere else. More accurately, one in which the tunes are openly *admitted* to have been stolen from somewhere else.

Ballet: A formal style of dance sometimes found in opera to give the singers a break from the music and the audience a break from the singers.

Bar: 1. A means of dividing music up into easily digested portions.
2. A means of providing musicians with easily digested portions of alcohol.

Baritone: Lying halfway between the bass and tenor ranges, the baritone is the middle-manager position of male voices — and often just about as useful. Found in opera singing such supporting roles as Old Man, Second Fool, Hero's Friend and so on. Rarely gets the girl.

Bartered Bride, The: An opera in three acts by Czech composer Bedrich Smetana. An earlier version, now lost, *The Battered Bride*, tells the tragic story of a clumsy waitress in a Prague pancake house.

Bass: The lowest voice, sung usually by men but sometimes by members of the former Soviet women's wrestling team. In opera, the bass is rarely the hero, but often sings an important role as villain or chief buffoon — either of which is ideally suited.

Bayreuth: (see Hell).

Beggar's Opera, The: A famous ballad opera with dialogue and verses by John Gay and music "arranged" (that is, stolen) by John Christopher

Pepusch. First performed, to enormous success, in London in 1728. Gay and Pepusch had less success with their little-known followup sequel, *The Beggars-Can't-Be-Choosers Opera*.

Bel Canto: A style of singing idealized in opera (from the Italian for "beautiful song") but rarely found there. Not to be confused with *Can belto*, an inferior style much more often encountered.

Belly: 1. In instruments such as the cello, the frontal curved surface over which the strings are stretched.
2. In singers, the frontal curved surface over which the shirt buttons are stretched.

Bow: 1. A slightly bent device for scraping sound out of a violin.
2. A slightly bent gesture for scraping sympathy out of an audience.

Bizet, Georges: A 19th-century French composer best known for the opera *Carmen*. Not to be confused with *bidet*, which is something else again.

Bladder-pipe: 1. An ancient instrument similar in sound and appearance to a bagpipe. Rarely found in opera.
2. A surgical device that would prove useful to those having to sit through unbearably long performances of opera.

Bore: 1. In brass and woodwind instruments, the term used to describe the passageway through

The Beggar's Opera

which air travels — generally either cylindrical or conical.

2. In opera singers, the term used to describe most of them.

Brünnhilde: In Norse mythology and Wagner's *Ring Cycle*, the daughter of Wotan and the leader of the Valkyries. A big, strapping blonde in a horned helmet and breastplate, she likes to come across as a tough, pushy broad. But at heart she's just Daddy's Little Girl.

Buffa: The Italian adjective meaning "comic." (See Opera Buffa.) As a noun, more often in the masculine form Buffo, it refers to the singer playing a comic role in an opera. Not to be confused with *boffo*, which is what producers want the box-office results to be.

C

Cadenza: An elaborate section at the end of an operatic aria, often improvised, in which singers get to show off the scales and exercises they've been practising for all these years. Not to be confused with *credenza*, a piece of furniture often far more beautiful and useful than anything a singer might possibly produce.

Cage, John: A 20th-century American composer known for highly experimental and unusual style. His famous piece *4'33"* consists entirely of silence — which would seem to make it ideally suited for adaptation as an opera (and at about the right length, too).

Carmen

Calore: An Italian musical term meaning "heat" or "passion." Not to be confused with *calories*, the energy value of food consumed in great quantities by opera singers.

Carmen: A popular opera by French composer Georges Bizet and the only one ever written about cigarette smugglers. Obviously composed before the introduction of federal laws and tough industry guidelines regulating undue glamorization of smoking and tobacco products.

Caruso, Enrico: A famous Italian operatic tenor of the late 19th and early 20th centuries who earned a worldwide reputation in heroic roles. No relation to Robinson Crusoe, the guy who washed up on a desert island, though some might have wanted them to trade places.

Castrato: A male singer surgically altered to retain the upper vocal range. The popularity of the *castrati* reached great heights (you should pardon the pun) in the18th-century operas of Handel, Porpora and others, even Mozart and Rossini. Now considered illegal in most civilized countries — and even America. They often played heroic roles and got the girl — but had no idea what to do with her.

Chest: A part of the human anatomy favored by some singers to produce a full, dark tone — and by others just to get attention.

Comic opera: The general term for operas with funny situations and happy endings. Despite the

Comic opera

name, they are not actually based on material from comic books, although in most cases the characters are no less cartoonish.

Compass: 1. Another term for the range of notes a singer is able to perform, from the lowest growl to the highest squeak.
2. A magnetic device that might give some singers the only way to arrive anywhere near the right notes.

Composer: The individual enormously important for creating the musical portion of an opera, whose importance all but vanishes once the opera gets

Counter-tenor

into production and into the hands of the director and conductor.

Conductor: The person at the front of the orchestra in the fancy tails, waving the little white stick and taking all the credit for everyone else's skill and hard work. Not to be confused with the conductor found on a train — although, like a railway conductor, once the thing gets under way, there's very little the music conductor will be able to do to stop it.

Contralto: A woman who sings the alto range, lower than soprano or mezzo-soprano, but (usually) higher than male tenors. Generally has more brains and fewer annoying mannerisms than any of the above singers, though sometimes has a tendency to sound muffled and thick, as though she were singing with a pillow over her face or a mouthful of peanut butter. In opera, the contralto sometimes gets to play the villainess, but more often gets stuck with such roles as Old Wise Woman, Mysterious Countess, Earth Mother and so on.

Counter-tenor: The highest adult male voice currently available through legal and moral means. Sings the alto range also covered by female contraltos, though rarely plays the same roles in opera (wouldn't fit into the costumes anyway). Without having to resort to radical surgery, counter-tenors are now sometimes used to re-create the *castrati* roles of Baroque operas. It's not entirely the same, but until someone is prepared to make the ultimate sacrifice of his personal life for the sake of art, it's about as close as we're going to get.

Crotchet: The English term for a quarter-note. Singers who perform too many of them are said to become crotchety.

Cruda sorte: 1. Isabella's aria at the opening of Rossini's *L'Italiana in Algeri*.
2. A term you might use to describe some of the tough guys on the production crew, or the jerks who hang around the stage door trying to pick up the singers.

Cue: 1. A gesture to indicate a musical entrance.
2. The long, tapered stick a musician might use

after a tough gig in a nice, relaxing game of pool.

D

Da capo: A type of operatic aria with a built-in encore, designed especially for those singers who might not otherwise get one. From the Italian for "the head." Singers who perform too many *da capo* arias are often said to have let fame go to their heads — hence the name.

Da Ponte, Lorenzo: An Italian writer chiefly remembered for librettos to Mozart operas *Le nozze di Figaro, Don Giovanni* and *Cosi fan tutte.* He later moved to New York and found a real job, as a grocer.

Daughter of the Regiment, The: An opera by Donizetti about a good-time party girl. The X-rated film version has yet to be released.

Dido's Lament: The famous soprano aria from the closing death scene of Purcell's *Dido and Aeneas.* The text begins "When I am laid in earth ..." Easily misconstrued by those who think it begins only "When I am laid" — which has a different meaning entirely.

Don

Discord: 1. Two or more notes that don't go well together.
2. The general atmosphere of most operatic companies, the result of two or more performers who don't go well together.

Diva: A fancy term for singer, especially the most important soprano(s) of a company — a matter of opinion (and fierce rivalry), of course. From the Italian for "goddess" — which unfortunately most of them take literally.

Dominant: 1. In harmonic theory, the fifth degree of the scale.
2. A personality type important for opera singers, and even more important for the conductor who must control them.

Don: A popular Italian first name (see Don Carlos, Don Giovanni, Don Ottavio, and so on).

Duet: A musical performance for two singers. Not to be confused with *duel*, which it often resembles.

E

Ear: An external auditory organ essential for hearing. Often present but sadly non-functional on many singers, especially of opera.

Embellishment: 1. A musical term for notes that are fancy addition(s) to an otherwise plain tune.
2. A cynical term for musicians who are fancy addition(s) to an otherwise plain group.

Encore: The repeat of a musical performance signifying (a) appreciation or (b) that it should be done again until the singer gets it right.

Execution: 1. A term used to describe the act of performing music: "I think the singer's execution of that phrase was marvelous."
2. A technique for dealing with singers who fail in the above endeavor: "I think the singer's execution would be a good idea — preferably by firing squad."

F

Falsetto: A vocal technique used by men to achieve notes in the highest range. Less permanent — and less painful — than that used for the *castrato* sound. The product of dedication, discipline, muscular control — or sometimes stepping the wrong way on a garden rake.

Farinelli: The stage name for Carlo Broschi, one of the greatest of the Italian *castrati* of the 18th century. After operatic triumphs in Italy and England, he retired early to the court of the King of Spain, where he relaxed playing harpsichord, collecting fine paintings and running the Madrid opera house — having nothing much better to do with his time.

Fedora: 1. A fancy opera written in 1898 by Umberto Giordano.
2. A fancy hat worn around the same time by Giuseppe Verdi.

Fermata: A pause in the music, useful as a sort of rallying point for getting back together if things are falling apart. Composers are well advised to include several, judiciously spaced throughout the score.

Fiddle: 1. A slang term for violin.
2. A slang term for what many unscrupulous impresarios do to the opera-house books.

Fidelio: Beethoven's famous opera about prison reform and marital fidelity — themes that have proven to be less than stellar draws at the box office (which may explain why it's Beethoven's only opera). The only opera in the repertoire with four overtures, three of them named *Leonore Overtures,* just to confuse matters. See the entry under Leonore, which might help explain things. Or it might not.

Figaro, The Marriage of: A popular comic opera by Mozart. Confusingly, does *not* contain the famous aria *"Figaro, Figaro, Figaro."* Some people refuse to believe this, and no amount of explaining will convince them otherwise.

Figure: 1. A small and recognizable grouping of notes.
2. The aspect of a singer's appearance that expands with time. (See Pasta.)

Florid: 1. The musical term for a passage with lots of extra notes.
2. The medical term for a performer's complexion after singing such a passage.

Form: See Figure.

Fret: 1. In guitars and other stringed instruments, small pieces of metal across the neck that make tuning easier.
2. In opera, the backstage activity akin to panic that results from realizing that no such devices exist to make the singer's tuning easier.

Fuguing Tune: 1. A type of simple, repetitive melody popular in 18th-century America.
2. In operas of Wagner, Lloyd Webber and others, an expression often heard when a simple, repetitive melody keeps coming back and won't go away, as in: "Do we have to listen to this fuguing tune again?!"

Fundamental discord: 1. In harmony, the name for a chord in which the discordant note is an

Marriage of Figaro

essential element (for example, the seventh in a dominant-seventh chord) and not just a passing note or a mistake.

2. The emotional state in which most opera companies operate.

G

Gay, John: An English poet and playwright of the 18th century, best remembered for providing the libretto to *The Beggar's Opera* in 1728. He warmed up for the job by writing the libretto for *Acis and Galatea*, by Handel, from whom *The Beggar's Opera* later stole some of its best tunes.

Gig: The musician's slang term for a job or performance. Not to be confused with *gigue*, a type of happy dance often performed by musicians who've just landed a gig.

Glissando: A kind of musical slide, often performed by opera singers in the theory that *one* of the notes along the way is bound to be right.

Gopak: See Hopak.

Götterdämmerung: 1. An opera by

Wagner. the fourth and last in the *Ring Cycle*.
2. An expression often heard from the audience of Wagner operas. (As in, "Isn't this *götterdämmerung* opera finished yet?")

Grand opera: The general term for serious operas, in which people die at the end. Distinguished from Comic opera, in which people get married at the end. In other words, one has a happy ending, the other a sad ending. You get to decide which is which.

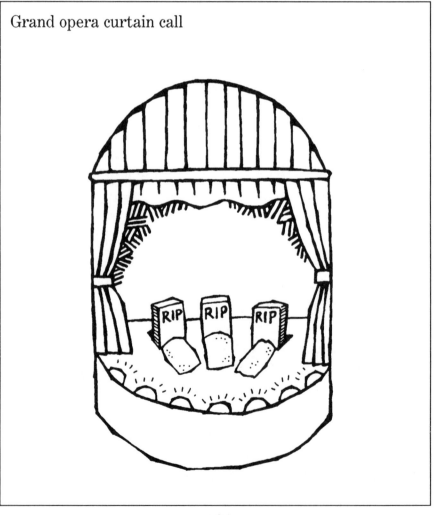

Grand opera curtain call

Guerre des Bouffons: The so-called "War of the Buffoons," an argument among the Paris elite of 1752 between supporters of the old-fashioned Italian style and newer French style of Rameau and others. Sparked by a revival performance of Pergolesi's *La serva padrona*, possibly just as a means of keeping it in the history books. The tradition survives today, in which buffoons continue to argue about opera.

H

Handel, G.F.: A German-born English Baroque composer of music in all genres, including such operas as *Acis and Galatea, Giulio Cesare, Rinaldo, Serse* and many others. Handel later abandoned operas when he found he couldn't earn a living composing them — a pragmatic example that many others would do well to follow.

Harmony: 1. The means of combining voices and/or instruments to the best and most pleasing musical effect.
2. The feeling of goodwill and benevolence that ought to exist among any group of singers or instrumentalists performing such music. It doesn't.

Head: 1. In singers, a term used to describe a particularly light and floating vocal tone.
2. In opera singers especially, the large and empty space above the neck that provides extra resonance.

Heldentenor: The German term for "heroic tenor," found in operas of Wagner and others, suitable for singers with bigger voices and even smaller brains than usual.

Hell: 1. A place of unending agony, torture and suffering often used as an operatic plot device (in *Don Giovanni, Faust, Orpheus in the Underworld* and many others).
2. Anything by Wagner.

Hopak: See Gopak.

I

Idyll: 1. A pleasant period of gentle peace and enjoyment. Not to be confused with an *opera*, which is pretty much the exact opposite.
2. In music, a short composition meant to portray such an event. Among the best known — and most surprising — of these is Wagner's *Siegfried Idyll*,

which includes themes from that opera.

Imbroglio: 1. In opera, the Italian term for a section of complicated music meant to suggest scheming, manipulation and confusion.
2. In most opera companies, the general state of affairs.

Iphegenia: In ancient Greek legend, a young woman with a lousy sense of direction (see *Iphegenia in Aulis, Iphegenia in Tauris,* and so on).

Impresario: The person who arranges all the details of presenting an opera production, in the hopes of *impressing* people. Possibly also related to the term *imprecise,* which describes the impresario's chance of actually predicting a production's success.

Italy: The cradle of the opera tradition, and the country still largely responsible for keeping it alive. All blame, complaints, class-action suits and other legal proceedings should be directed there.

J

Jaw: A portion of the human facial anatomy useful to opera singers especially for articulation, enumerating contract demands and breaking (better that it be someone else's) when such contract demands are not met.

Jazz: A style of music occasionally found in (for example, *Porgy and Bess*), and in any case infinitely superior to, the standard opera repertoire.

Jewels: Articles of adornment often worn by opera singers both on stage and off. Although many of them may be precious family heirlooms, these should not be confused with *family jewels*, which in the case of the *castrati* have been removed.

K

Key: 1. A complex, unfathomable term to describe the interrelationship of notes in a given piece or section of music.
2. A device for opening doors at an opera house (not to be confused with *bribe*).

Key Signature: 1. In musical notation, the arrangement of sharps or flats at the beginning of the score to denote the key (see Key).
2. In professional negotiations, the essential or most important signature on a contract or pay stub.

Keyboard: A type of instrument (piano, harpsichord and so on), used to accompany opera performances, especially in rehearsal. Not to be confused with *key bored*, a sign that the composer should consider a modulation.

L

Lablache, Luigi: A famous 19th-century Italian bass, celebrated for performances as Leporello in Mozart's *Don Giovanni*, the title role in Donizetti's *Don Pasquale*, and many others. Sang at the funerals of Haydn, Beethoven and Chopin. Maybe he was a jinx.

La donna è mobile: The well-known tenor aria from Verdi's *Rigoletto* in which the Duke of Mantua relates his attitude toward women. Roughly translated from the Italian (well, very roughly), the phrase means: "Boy, look at that woman move!"

Largo al factotum: Figaro's famous patter song from the opening of Rossini's *Barber of Seville* in which he lists his many duties and responsibilities. Seen by many as an early form of labor-relations contract, though considered less binding in a court of law.

Largo, Handel's: The popular name given to

instrumental arrangements of a famous aria from Handel's opera *Serse*. The term is inaccurate, since the passage itself is actually marked *Larghetto*, which is still slow, but a little faster than *Largo*. (But somehow *Handel's Larghetto* just doesn't have the right ring to it.) In the opera, the aria, *Ombra mai fù*, is the hero's passionate address to a big tree — which may explain why it so often gets such a wooden performance.

Laryngitis: A physical affliction affecting singers that results in partial or total loss of vocal ability. (As opposed to loss of musical ability, which is a whole different affliction, often congenital.) Less permanent and so less effective than either drastic surgery or death. Depending on your perspective, it may be seen as either a curse or a blessing — maybe even a form of divine retribution.

Leer: 1. A musical term from the German for "empty." It can refer to open strings of the violin or similar instruments and sometimes to the intellectual capacity (or bank accounts) of operatic singers.
2. The look one opera singer will sometimes give another. Often followed by a slap or rude remark.

Leitmotiv: From the German for "leading motif," a fancy highbrow term to describe recurring little signature tunes that in opera may be associated with a particular character, object, idea or place. The 19th-century equivalent of today's radio and TV commercial jingles, though neither as clever nor entertaining. Often misspelled "leitmotif," a

Laryngitis

piece of information useful for detecting and deflating pretentious musical snobs (there is no other kind).

Mozart, Weber, Berlioz and other composers have used leitmotivs, but the practice is most often associated with Wagner — who in the *Ring Cycle* went a little nuts on the subject, actually. (It was a short trip.) For reasons no one quite understands, Wagner preferred the term *hauptmotiv*, but history has overruled him on the issue. (Unfortunately, it wasn't able to overrule him on many others.)

Leonore: The heroine of Beethoven's only opera, and one of the few happily and faithfully married characters in the entire operatic repertoire. Beethoven wrote four *Leonore* overtures, all of them for an opera he then called *Fidelio*. Go figure. The fourth is now generally the one played to start the opera and so is called the *Fidelio Overture*. *Leonore No. 3* is often performed to introduce the final act. *Leonores 1* and *2* didn't make the cut.

Leporello: The faithful servant (bass) to the hero in Mozart's *Don Giovanni*. He sings the famous *Catalogue Aria* (*Madamina! il catalogo è questo*) in the opening scene, bragging about the number of his boss's romantic conquests. (This was long before Political Correctness. Nowadays his account would be considered part of a Victim Impact Statement.) Just for the record, Leporello lists 640 in Italy, 231 in Germany, an even 100 in France, a mere 91 in Turkey and an astounding 1,003 in Spain (where Don Giovanni obviously had the home-court advantage), for a grand total of 2,065. But considering the number Don Giovanni actually succeeds with in his own opera (i.e. zilch), it's probably fair to assume that Leporello is exaggerating just a bit — basking in his master's reflected glory, obviously.

Libiamo: The famous drinking song in the opening

act of Verdi's *La Traviata*. An instance of officially sanctioned drinking on stage — as opposed to the drinking in most other operas, which takes place off in the wings or the dressing room.

La, la, la,...

Libretto: In opera, the term for the lyrics and dialogue that make up the story. From the Italian for "little book," a useful reminder to the prudent operagoer to bring along a good book to read in case the opera itself is a deadly bore.

Lohengrin: A famous Wagner opera about a bunch of heroic knights. Possibly based on a much earlier work, later discarded — *Low 'n' Green*, about a bunch of heroic frogs.

Lothario: 1. In Thomas's opera *Mignon*, a wandering old minstrel who turns out to be a nobleman.
2. In other operas in general, any old musician with wandering hands who turns out to be far from noble.

M

Mad Scene: A common operatic plot device that allows singers (usually sopranos) to display elaborate vocal technique, dramatic skill and their true personality type. Found in such operas as Berg's *Lulu* and Donizetti's *Anna Bolena* and *Lucia di Lammermoor*. Also frequently found off stage when contracts are being renewed.

Maestro: An affectionate nickname (from the Italian "master") for the conductor of operas and other musical productions. Used in public and polite company, as opposed to the other nicknames often given to conductors — most of which are unprintable in a book aimed at general audiences.

Magic Flute, The: Mozart's famous and popular opera about the triumph of true love over dangers that include a deadly dragon, a vengeful mother-in-law, mystical magic spells and one really loopy guy in a bird suit.

Mass: 1. A term to describe the central religious ceremony of the Christian church, for which generations of composers have provided music. References to it are sometimes found in opera, as in the opening scene of Mascagni's *Cavalleria rusticana*.

2. A term to describe the overall bulk of singers, which seems to increase as their careers progress. (See Pasta.)

Melba, Nellie: An Australian coloratura soprano of the late 19th and early 20th centuries who became so popular she had not one but two food dishes named after her: Peach Melba and Melba toast. Appropriate symbolism, really, since singers whose careers aren't peachy just end up as toast.

Melody: That aspect of music most often sacrificed to a singer's ego. (But see also Rhythm.)

Mezza voce: From the Italian for "half-voice," a technique of singing more quietly. In most opera singers, this reduces the tone from the ear-splitting to the merely uncomfortable.

Mezzo-soprano: A kind of half-hearted soprano, with fewer of the high notes but also generally fewer of the temper tantrums. In opera, sometimes plays the heroine but more often is just a sidekick.

Mime: In general, a term for a performer who remains entirely silent. In Wagner's *Ring Cycle*, the name of one of the Nibelung dwarfs, the brother of Alberich and foster father of Siegfried. Operas in general, and Wagner's in particular, ought to have more mimes — at least the kind who shut up and don't sing.

Mad scene

Modern music: The mess we're in now. A polite term people use when they don't know what else to call it. (See Noise.)

Modulation: The movement from one key to another, generally (but not always) a related key. Modulation often proceeds upwards by semitones, a technique good orchestras may find useful in keeping up with an opera singer let loose in a cadenza.

Monody: A compositional style for single voice and accompaniment developed in Italy in the early 16th century by Caccini and members of the Florentine Camerata. An early stage in the development of opera. Not to be confused with *monotony*, which comes in the later stages.

Monteverdi, Claudio: An influential and prolific Italian composer (1567-1643) considered by many (except friends and family of Caccini, Peri and that crowd) to be the "father" of opera. Any class-action (or paternity) suits should be directed to the Monteverdi estate.

Motives: 1. The plural of *motiv* (sometimes *motif*), the name for a short melodic phrase or fragment used by composers to establish thematic material. Often called melodic motives.
2. Impulses that drive musicians to certain, usually selfish, behaviors. Often called ulterior motives.

Mozart, Wolfgang Amadeus: Child prodigy and musical genius of the 18th century, put on Earth as

Claudio Monteverdi

DEAR OLD DAD

God's way of making the rest of us feel insignificant. A superb composer in all forms and genres, even his operas — *The Magic Flute, The Marriage of Figaro, Don Giovanni* and others — are wonderful and good fun, too (just to prove that it can work when it's done right).

Muse: In ancient Greek myth, one of several beautiful women who took credit for inspiring poets, musicians and other creative types — but who, unfortunately, never stuck around to take the blame if their inspirations didn't work out. In this respect, they are the forerunners of the modern-day opera company artistic directors who get fired or jump ship between seasons, so they don't have to stick around to see their elaborate and unworkable plans fall to ruins.

Music: 1. Any assortment of noises, sounds and occasional silences assembled into something resembling an organized structure. (In the case of Modern music, it's mostly just noise, and the organization is hardly worth mentioning.)
2. In printed form, any assortment of obscure lines, dots, curves, squiggles and blotches assembled into something resembling an organized score. (Again, in Modern music, it's mostly just the blotches and squiggles, with very few of the lines, dots and curves.)

Music drama: A term often used throughout history in place of opera (in Italian, *dramma per musica*), and the term preferred by Wagner to describe the mammoth, bloated spectacles he inflicted on his unsuspecting audiences. (Although you'd think, after the first one, they'd have started to catch on.)

Musical: 1. The adjective pertaining to music, used to describe a state or quality that embodies music.
2. In modern theatre, the term to describe the popular successor of the operatic form, a production on Broadway or elsewhere that includes singers, dancers and instrumentalists in a comic

or dramatic story told in music. The most success-ful composer of the modern musical is Andrew Lloyd Webber, whose works include *Cats*, *Evita* and *Phantom of the Opera*.

3. In many such Broadway-style shows, the essential quality some productions lack. Ironically, many musicals are hardly musical at all.

Musician: A person with knowledge and skill in music employed to perform it. ("Employed" often only in the figurative, not literal, sense — which is to say the money that's supposed to change hands rarely does.) The debate continues over whether singers should really be considered musicians at all (see reference to "knowledge and skill," above).

N

Nabucco: See Nebuchadnezzar.

Nadir: 1. One of the pearl fishers, a tenor, in Bizet's opera *Les Pêcheurs de Perles*. 2. A scientific term to describe the lowest possible point, the bottom, the deepest pit in the ocean and so on.

3. In opera, a term to describe the level of quality reached by some productions, or the place it might be best to put them.

Natural: 1. In musical terminology, a note that has neither a flat nor sharp.
2. In opera, an adjective used to describe a style of performing (acting or singing) much admired and rarely obtained. (See Wooden.)

Nebuchadnezzar: 1. An ancient Babylonian king, the title character of Verdi's opera *Nabucco* (the Italian spelling's easier).
2. A very large bottle of champagne, larger than a magnum, suitable for consuming after an opera (especially Verdi).

Neck: 1. The long, narrow part of many stringed instruments (violin, ukulele and others) that joins the pegboard to the soundbox.
2. The shorter, thicker part of many singers suitable for wringing when they botch a performance (or just on general principles).

Nibelungen: A class of dwarfs known chiefly to inhabit the operas of Wagner, where they fashion magic rings and helmets, raise orphans and hang around damp caves. Despite extensive vocation counselling, no more productive occupation has yet been found for them.

Noise: Disorganized sound — as opposed to music, which is organized sound. Sometimes, especially in opera (see Wagner), it's hard to tell the difference.

In some Modern music, there is no difference.

Notes: 1. The little circles, sticks and flags that composers put on paper to convey their ideas to performers. (I find such naivete charming, don't you?) Although in theory such notation is actually quite precise, in practice the two events — notation and performance — are often miles apart. (In the case of Canadian or European performances, kilometres.) In each case there is a great matter of pride involved. Composers take pride in notating their ideas as accurately as possible, and performers take pride in ignoring them as "artistically" as possible. 2. In opera, notes are also reminders of interpretation, stage direction and so on that a director will give to performers during rehearsals. These are likewise ignored.

Nuance: A degree of subtlety (in interpretation, gesture, performance) entirely beyond the capabilities of most operatic performers, and indeed of most operatic composers.

O

Obbligato: The fancy Italian term composers use to designate that a certain instrument must be used in a particular passage. The musical equivalent of a binding contract. Interestingly, the term is rarely if ever applied to specific singing voices. (Composers may be demanding, but they're not stupid.)

Octave: In harmonic theory, an interval of eight steps or degrees. In the real world of opera singers, (if you can call that the real world), your guess is as good as mine — or theirs.

Opera: An overrated production in which overweight performers sing overblown music in overpriced theatres for overlong periods of time. Actually, the stereotype that all opera singers are fat, stupid and arrogant is hardly fair. Some of them have lost weight recently.

Opera buffa: Not, as you might expect, opera in the nude. Not yet, anyway. Not to be confused with *opera buffet,* a little party that comes after the performance.

Opera lover: A person who believes that nothing succeeds like excess.

Operetta: A less serious or pretentious form of opera designed for popular entertainment. A kind of calorie-reduced Opera Lite, with less fat and generally easier to digest.

Orchestra: A bunch of instrumentalists larger than an ensemble but smaller (and usually less dangerous) than an army. In opera, it's the gang down in

Opera buffa

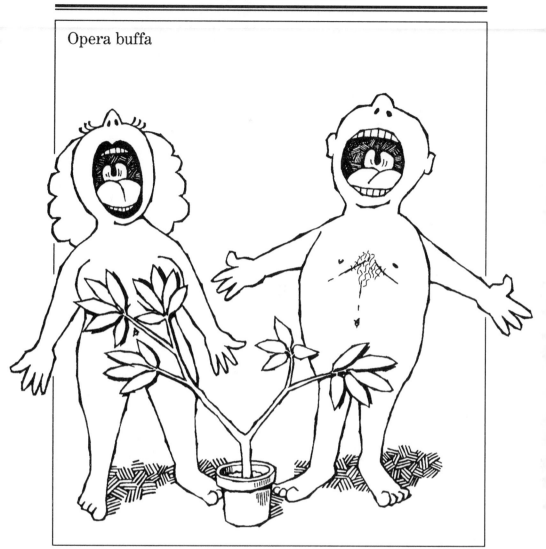

the pit trying desperately to drown out the singers.

Orfeo: A character from Greek myth, husband of Euridice, and a central role in several operas, including the earliest by Peri and Monteverdi, and later ones by Gluck, Offenbach and others. A musician and a bit of a whiner, actually, and prone to wandering around the nether regions without

Ornaments

many clothes on (see Offenbach's *Orpheus in his Underwear*). Not to be confused with *Oreo*, which is a kind of cookie.

Orlofsky, Prince: A "pants role" in Johann Strauss's *Die Fledermaus*, usually sung by a mezzo, the kind who nowadays might appear on an afternoon talk show. ("Women who dress up like men and crash parties." "I'm a mezzo trapped in a baritone's body." "My husband lets me wear the pants in the family.") See Travesti.

Ornaments: 1. The term for the fancy bits that dress up an otherwise plain piece of music.
2. The term for the fancy bits who dress up an otherwise plain chorus line or orchestra.

Overblown: 1. In wind instruments, a term to describe higher notes than should normally be produced.
2. In opera, a term to describe an excessively elaborate performance or production, often one involving higher notes than should normally be produced.

Overtures: 1. Instrumental pieces that introduce operas.
2. Romantic advances that introduce opera performers to each other.

P

Pagliacci, I: The famous tragic opera by Leoncavallo with a bunch of clowns on stage. Or rather, the famous opera in which all the clowns on stage are actually meant to be there.

Pang: 1. A tenor role in Puccini's *Turandot*.
2. A kind of stomach pain suffered by singers, often those attempting Puccini tenor roles.

Pants role: See Travesti.

Papagena and Papageno: Silly young lovers in Mozart's *The Magic Flute* — the Mutt and Jeff, Frick and Frack, Burns and Allen of the operatic world.

Parlando: In opera, a style of singing that's closer to speaking — as opposed to the usual style, which is closer to screaming.

Parsifal: The hero and title character of one of Wagner's operas, a noble medieval knight sent on a sacred Grail quest and described in the story as a "guileless fool." It's a tenor role, obviously.

Partial: 1. In the study of acoustics, a term to

describe each multiple of a fundamental vibration.

2. In opera productions, a term to describe the biased attitude of a casting director.

3. In opera singers, a term to describe that portion of brain capacity they are capable of using (also known as *negligible*).

Passion: A highly emotional state often required by opera composers on stage and demonstrated by opera singers off stage.

Pasta, Giuditta: An Italian operatic soprano of the early 19th century, celebrated for creating such roles as Bellini's *Norma* and *La Sonnambula* and Donizetti's *Anna Bolena*. In her honor, opera singers consume enormous amounts of pasta each year.

Perfect Fool, The: 1. A one-act opera by Gustav Holst, first performed in 1923.

2. A name for anyone who willingly attends an opera performance, especially of Wagner.

Piano: 1. A keyboard instrument useful for accompanying operatic performances, especially in rehearsal.

2. A dynamic level, quite quiet, most opera singers find it almost impossible to achieve. And for them, the next quietest dynamic level, *pianissimo*, is entirely a theoretical concept.

Prima donna: The most important female performer of an opera or opera company, or anyone who thinks she is — which is pretty much everybody. Not to be confused with *pre-Madonna*, that time period before the arrival of the pop star who elevated prima donna-ish behavior to an art form.

Principals: In an opera company or production, the term for the most important performers or singing roles. Not to be confused with *principles*, a set of moral guidelines often entirely lacking in such performers, and also in impresarios at contract time.

Quality: A desirable state rarely attained in operatic performances.

Quartet: What's left of most orchestras after the

Queen of the Night

latest round of funding cutbacks.

Quasi: A term from the Italian meaning "almost" or "as if." Thus Beethoven's *"Moonlight" Sonata, quasi una fantasia* — almost a fantasia. This term often applies to operas, which involve a lot of quasi-singing (if that's what you want to call it) to deliver something only somewhat close to what the composer intended — a quasi-*Figaro*, quasi-*Bohème*, quasi-*Pagliacci* or whatever.

Quaver: 1. The English term for the eighth-note.
2. What nervous singers do before an opera performance, especially one involving a lot of eighth-notes.

Queen of the Night: 1. A fearsome, domineering and imperious woman, Pamina's mother, in Mozart's *The Magic Flute*.
2. Any fearsome, domineering and imperious soprano who sings the role.
3. Just about any singer you could name, usually female.

R

Racket: 1. In Renaissance music, the name for a particular woodwind instrument with a very low range.
2. In Modern music, the best word to describe most of what you hear.

Rank: 1. In church organs, a means of distinguishing one set of pipes from another, and a method of establishing their relative importance to the overall sound.
2. In opera companies, the same thing.

Rant: 1. In the 17th century, a kind of dance performed in England, accompanied by instruments. 2. In the 20th century, a kind of tirade performed off stage, often in dressing rooms or manager's offices, accompanied by threats and imperious demands.

Recital: A place where old opera singers go before they die. Sometimes they die there, too.

Recitative: In opera, a musical device for leading from one aria to the next to create a seamless whole (sometimes hole) — the musical equivalent of tile grouting or the wiring that strings together the lights on a Christmas tree. Recitatives (or "recits") are delivered in a style that combines singing with speaking and evokes the negative qualities of both. They are useful for conveying information (as distinct from arias, which convey only emotion or self-indulgence). *Recitativo accompagnato*, or *stromentato*, accompanies the singer with several orchestral instruments. Recits featuring the singer with only harpsicord and perhaps a bass instrument (cello, bassoon, double-Bflat contrakazoo or whatever) are called *recitative secco*, from the Italian for "dry" (as opposed to the arias — which, with all that sobbing, are considerably more soggy).

Realism: A concept theoretically desirable but practically never obtainable in opera. See Verismo.

Relative: 1. In harmony, a term for describing the association of two keys.
2. In opera, a person you can usually depend upon

(or at least bribe) to attend your premiere.

Rescue opera: 1. A genre of opera especially popular in 18th-century France with plotlines in which the hero and heroine escape from disastrous situations.
2. What someone should do to the whole art form before it goes completely down the tubes.

Resonance: The acoustical property of air filling space, adding "body" and "warmth" to the sound being produced. With instruments, the amount of resonance is determined mostly by the size and capacity of the instrument itself. With singers, especially opera singers, resonance can be increased by expanding the chest cavity, and by moving the tone up into the head, to allow extra resonance in the empty space where the brain normally would be.

Rest: 1. A brief period of relative calm in a piece of music — usually intentional but sometimes just a way of shutting up until you can figure out what's going on around you.
2. What some of us need after being subjected to long performances, especially of opera.
3. The kind of home old opera singers should be sent to when they're past their prime.

Rheingold, Das: An elaborate opera by Wagner, the first of four that make up the *Ring Cycle*. Notable as the only opera in the standard repertoire to take place under water, which helps explain why it sounds so bloated, soggy and generally washed up.

Das Rheingold

Rhythm: 1. A complicated mathematical method of preventing collisions and unwanted overlaps in music.
2. An even more complicated reproductive method of preventing unwanted musicians.

Ring Cycle: The popular English name for the four

operas of Wagner's *Der Ring des Nibelungen*. Not to be confused with the Rinse Cycle, which is what you put your clothes through after sitting through an entire performance of Wagner's operas.

Ring des Nibelungen, Der: A massive four-opera cycle by Richard Wagner about a bunch of dwarfs, giants and spiteful Norse gods running around stealing each other's treasure and fighting over a magic decoder ring. (Imagine a bunch of kids arguing over the prize in a specially marked popcorn box. Now imagine that at six times the volume and with a full orchestra. Got the idea?)

Rossini, Gioacchino: One of the nicer of the big-name opera composers, an 18th-century Italian whose works include *The Barber of Seville*, *William Tell* and *The Thieving Magpie*. Enormously successful and popular (and just plain enormous, too), Rossini knew enough to quit while he was ahead — a bit of wisdom very few other composers have managed to acquire.

Round: 1. A simple, repetitive piece of music popular in nursery rhymes and sometimes found in opera.
2. The general shape of most opera singers by the time their careers are established. (See Figure.)

Runs: 1. Long passages of notes that allow singers to show off the hours they've spent practising scales.
2. An intestinal disorder singers hope won't occur on stage, especially during those long passages of

Rossini

Runs

notes while they're showing off their scales.

S

Sagbut: 1. A brass instrument (also spelled sackbut), an early form of trombone, rarely found in opera performances.
2. A condition bound to afflict aging opera singers

unless they get regular exercise.

Sainete: A form of comic opera popular in late 18th-century Spain, generally involving scenes with lowlife characters. Distinct from modern productions, where most of the lowlifes are either part of the production crew or in management.

Salieri, Antonio: An Italian composer of operas and other genres working in 18th-century Vienna. Hugely popular in his own day but largely forgotten now except as the man who supposedly poisoned Mozart. Rimsky-Korsakov wrote a whole opera about him, based on a poem by Pushkin. Salieri didn't actually poison Mozart (the fact that Mozart had health problems and later bought the farm is pretty much his own fault) but that hardly makes the story less entertaining. It just goes to show, you should take your fame wherever you can get it.

Salome: A Biblical "bad girl" and the title character of Richard Strauss's operatic adaptation of the famous Oscar Wilde play. Does the *Dance of the Seven Veils* and gets the head of John the Baptist served up on a platter (so not the kind of girl you'd want to take home to Mother). Not to be confused with *salami* — which, although likewise often served up on a platter, is generally considered more appropriate dinnertime fare.

Sanglot: A fancy French term for "sob," the kind of cheap, theatrical device opera singers often resort to, especially if they can't remember the words.

Salome

Scale: 1. The stepwise motion of notes a singer must master before moving on to the operatic or concert repertoire.
2. The rate of pay the union demands for a singer who has mastered such material.

Scat: 1. A style of singing found especially in jazz, characterized by rapid nonsense syllables.
2. A command for getting rid of unwanted animals, and sometimes singers repeating rapid nonsense syllables.

Scene: 1. The setting or location of the action in a passage of opera. Composers try to include them to make the drama flow more smoothly.
2. A period of great discomfort and enormous tactical advantage created by a singer dissatisfied with the current rate of pay, size of dressing room, billing on the marquee or whatever. Managers try to avoid them to make the production flow more smoothly.

Schweigsame Frau, Die: A comic opera (*The Silent Woman*) by Richard Strauss, first performed in Dresden in 1935. In my opinion, the world of opera would benefit greatly from having a whole lot more silent women (and men, too).

Score: 1. The various parts of a musical composition gathered together in one place for easy perusal or disposal.
2. What some of the singers hope to do with some of the other singers before the production is over.

Serse: The hero and title character of Handel's only

comic opera. He gets to sing his big love song (*Ombra mai fù*) to a tree — which isn't actually as funny as it sounds, but it is pretty amusing. (For more fascinating information on this topic, see Largo, Handel's)

Serva padrona, La: A little intermezzo written by Pergolesi in 1733 that's considered absolutely crucial to the development of *opera buffa* in the 18th century. Everybody says so, so it must be true. Pay attention, this might be on the exam.

Shake: 1. In early music, another name for Trill.
2. In opera, an attack of nerves singers succumb to before going on stage (and sometimes while on stage).

Sharp: 1. A term for describing a note (intentionally or otherwise) that has been slightly raised in pitch.
2. A term for describing a colleague's new outfit.
3. What managers and agents have to be to stay ahead of the game.

Siegfried: The hero and title character of the third opera in Wagner's *Ring Cycle*. Siegfried is the illegitimate son of an incestuous liaison between a twin brother and sister, Siegmund and Sieglinde, who got it on together in the previous opera, *Die Walküre*. (This is the kind of thing that drives the "family values" types to hysterics — admittedly a short trip.)

Singer: The person employed (figuratively and

Sharp

sometimes literally) to bring a composer's work to life on the opera stage. Singers come in various shapes and sizes, with a variety of vocal ranges and, unfortunately, an even greater variety of skill (generally from negligible at worst to moderate at best). Composers have not yet found a way to produce operas or other vocal music without having to resort to singers — but they're working on it.

Sleepwalking: 1. An operatic plot device (most notably in Bellini's *La sonnambula*) and a useful ruse for leaving a bad production early, if you can get away with it.

Snob: Another word for operagoer.

Soprano: The female singer with the highest vocal and salary range. In opera, sopranos are usually the heroines, and sometimes also the heroine's best friend, faithful servant, long-lost sister or whatever. Generally pretty clueless, the soprano's main job is to stand around looking good while others fight over her. Sometimes gets to die in the end — tragically and at great length.

Sotto voce: An Italian term (literally "under the voice") directing performers to sing very quietly. With most opera singers, this means turning down the volume so it doesn't actually peel paint off the walls, just loosens it a bit.

Stop: 1. In stringed instruments, the action of pressing down on a string to determine its pitch.
2. In church organs, a knob you pull out to change from one sound to another, hardly any better than the first.
3. In operas, what you wish the singers would do long before they actually get around to it.

T

Takt: The German term for "beat" or "measure," meaning the underlying pulse of a piece of music. Not to be confused with *tact*, meaning an essential quality of diplomacy and consideration that most musicians lack.

Tantrum: An emotional display of temper, impatience and selfishness, invoked when reason fails to attain the desired goal. A favorite device of children and singers (a needless distinction) who want to get their own way. Like children, singers often find that if a tantrum doesn't work, two tantrums usually does.

Temperament: 1. An aspect in the tuning of keyboard and other instruments that must be delicately balanced and manipulated to produce a pleasing sound.
2. An aspect in the personality of opera singers and other performers that must be delicately balanced and manipulated to produce a pleasing sound. Compared to singers, doing it to keyboards is a snap.

Tempo: The pace of a piece of music, generally

either too slow or too fast. Tempo is established in two stages — first by indications on the printed score and then by the actual performance itself. The two rarely have anything to do with each other.

Tenor: A male singer with a high voice and an even higher opinion of himself. In comic opera, the tenor usually gets to play the hero, adored by the people and lucky in the romance department. This can lead to problems off stage, where tenors mistakenly assume the same privileges still apply. In tragic opera, the tenor still gets to play the hero but rarely gets the girl, because either one or other of them dies, sometimes both. (Strangely, they never seem to feel this privilege should apply off stage as well. Too bad.)

Tie: 1. In musical notation, a device for linking one note to another.
2. At a performance, a decorative article of clothing, prone to attracting spills at intermission.
3. In vocal duets, the only diplomatic way to decide the winner.

Time: 1. An important aspect of musical notation. (See Tempo.)
2. One of the four dimensions of the universe, which physicists theorize moves forward at a constant pace. Audience members and musicians, especially those stuck listening to (or worse, performing in) bad operas, know this not to be true. There, time may drag to a near standstill (or pass quite quickly once you've fallen asleep). Obviously,

Travesti

the full effect of opera, especially bad opera, on Einstein's General Theory of Relativity has yet to be studied.

Touch: 1. In keyboard and other instruments, a part of the action that contributes to tone quality.
2. In rehearsal or performance, the kind of action

that can get you in trouble if unwelcome or misinterpreted.

Travesti: The Italian term for the so-called "pants role" in which a female singer plays a male character (this rarely happens the other way around), such as Romeo in Bellini's *I Capuletti*, Smeton in Donizetti's *Anna Bolena*, Cherubino in Mozart's *Marriage of Figaro* and so on. Not to be confused with *travesty*, a term that refers to all operas in general.

Triangle: 1. A small but obnoxiously loud percussion instrument.
2. The sort of romantic entanglement often essential to the dramatic narrative of operas, and often equally unavoidable off stage as well (though not always in the same combinations).

Trill: 1. A minor earthquake in the region of a particular note, said to be ornamental, but often merely a substitute for accuracy. Opera singers are especially fond of trilling, since it saves them the bother of having to learn the tunes properly.

Tune: A simple melody created by a composer and then butchered by performers.

Tuning: 1. A means by which orchestras establish harmonic consensus — largely as a result of compromise, sometimes bribery or coercion.
2. An abstract concept with which singers have very little firsthand knowledge.

U

Unessential notes: 1. In musical theory, any notes between harmonic chords, such as passing notes or suspensions, and considered less important than the notes that form the main harmonic and melodic material.

2. In opera, just about all of them.

Upbeat: 1. A conductor's motion that prepares for a rhythmic accent.

2. What conductors must remain to encourage their performers, even when things are falling apart (often the result of conductors forgetting to make the right motions to prepare for rhythmic accents).

Upright: 1. A style of piano, smaller than a grand, found in homes and rehearsal halls.

2. What singers and audiences should remain for the duration of an opera.

V

Valhalla: 1. In Norse mythology, the abode of the gods up in the sky and the final reward for heroic warriors. A place of wine, women, song, feasting and merriment — pretty much like a Legion hall on a rowdy Saturday night, but with mead and swordplay instead of beer and poker.
2. In Wagner's *Ring Cycle*, the elaborate palace built in the first opera (*Das Rheingold*) for Wotan and Fricka by the giants Fasolt and Fafner. Like most contractors, they end up haggling over the final price, and they aren't around in the end when the whole thing falls apart from bad workmanship.

Valkyrie: 1. In Norse mythology, one of a troop of fierce warrior women on flying horses, an early and impressive example of affirmative action in the military — a kind of militant cleaning lady on steroids. Ferocious but tidy, the Valkyries protect warriors in battle and, when they goof up, carry away the dead to Valhalla, keeping the battlefield from getting too cluttered. In *Die Walküre* and the rest of Wagner's *Ring Cycle*, the Valkyries are led by Brünnhilde, a moody but endearingly loyal pyromaniac with a strong Joan of Arc complex.

Variations: 1. Intentional alterations to the original version of a tune by which composers display their inventive cleverness.

2. Accidental alterations to a tune by which performers, especially opera singers, display their arrogance and disrespect for composers. In practice, every operatic aria is a variation, since singers consider that performing it the same way each time would be a sign of weakness.

Verismo: A stylistic movement of the late 19th century, typified by Leoncavallo's *I Pagliacci* and others, based on the laughable premise that operas

Valhalla

FIRE SALE!

Votre toast

should attempt to become more realistic or truthful. A movement doomed to failure, because of the inherent contradiction of the premise.

Vibrato: A vocal wobble, the musical equivalent of those restaurant tables with one leg just slightly shorter than the others — and just about as annoying, too.

Voice: An opera singer's chief instrument of commanding respect, whether on stage singing or off stage demanding a larger dressing room.

Votre toast: 1. The name of Escamillo's famous *Toreador Song* in Act II of Bizet's *Carmen*.
2. Having spent the night with a cute French singer, what you might offer in the morning for breakfast.

W

Wagner: 1. A student character in various operatic versions of the Faust legend. (See Hell.)
2. A German composer, Richard Wagner, of long, overblown operas. (See Hell.)

Walküre, Die: See Brünnhilde, Valkyrie.

Wind Machine: A large, barrel-shaped device for imitating the sound of rushing wind. Used by composers such as Richard Strauss in his tone-poem *Don Quixote* and, of course, in the person of all opera singers.

Wooden: In opera, an adjective to describe the construction material of some of the instruments and the acting style of most of the singers.

Words: Essential elements for conveying mood, narrative and emotion. In opera, carefully chosen by librettists and wantonly disregarded by singers.

Wotan: The chief god in Norse mythology and a central character in Wagner's *Ring Cycle*. A demanding but inspiring leader but at heart a doting father, some musicologists see Wotan as representing the absent father figure whom Wagner longed for in his own life. Far too Freudian and weird to think about — a topic best avoided altogether.

X

Xenophobia: The irrational mistrust and dislike of foreigners — a condition that might result from watching too many operas.

Xerxes: The hero of one of Handel's operas and a man with a seriously weird tree obsession. It's a *castrato* role, which may or may not have anything to do with it — depending how much faith you put in Freud. (See Serse.)

Xylophone: A percussion instrument that in both

Zauberoper

appearance and sound resembles a pile of old kindling. Mozart used a glockenspiel, a metallic version of the instrument, for the birdy stuff in *The Magic Flute*, but otherwise the xylophone doesn't show up much in opera. Wagner might have found a use for it in the *Ring Cycle*, if only for lighting Brünnhilde's funeral pyre.

Y

Yodelling: A bizarre form of vocal warbling found in certain regions of the Swiss Alps during traditional ceremonies and on opera stages all the time.

Z

Zaide: An unfinished opera by Mozart — which, had he completed it, would have been more interesting to scholars and more useful for the purposes of this dictionary.

Zarzuela: A fancy Spanish term for short operettas, usually comic but sometimes tragic, and a useful word for impressing your friends at your next cocktail party.

Zauberflöte, Die: See Magic Flute, The.

Zauberoper: A German term ("magic opera") for operas with supernatural or unbelievable elements: fire-breathing dragons, magic spells, honest politicians — whatever.

Zitti, zitti: 1. A trio sung by Almaviva, Figaro and Rosina in Act II of Rossini's *The Barber of Seville*. 2. A facial outbreak that's going to put a damper on your hopes for a big date.

Zukunftsmusik: A highfalutin German word meaning "music of the future," the term often used by Wagner and his followers to describe his music. A depressing concept, really. If Wagner's operas represent the music of the future, what's the point in going on?

Zzzz: The sound of contentment made by opera singers after a taxing performance, and by audiences during. Especially prevalent in operas by Wagner and those really weird modern composers.

ABOUT THE AUTHOR

David Barber is a journalist and musician and the author of five previous humorous books about music. Formerly the entertainment editor of the Kingston *Whig-Standard*, he now divides his time between working as an entertainment copyeditor at the Toronto *Globe and Mail* and, with his wife, Judy Scott, operating their bookstore/café, White Knight Books and The Dormouse Café, in Westport, Ont. As a composer, his works include two symphonies, a jazz mass based on the music of Dave Brubeck, a *Requiem*, several short choral works and numerous vocal-jazz arrangements. In his spare time he is an avid kayaker and reader of mysteries and enjoys performing with his vocal-jazz group, Barber and the Sevilles.

ABOUT THE ILLUSTRATOR

Dave Donald can't remember when he didn't scrawl his little marks on most surfaces, so it doesn't come as much of a surprise that he now makes a living doing just that. He is currently freelancing his way through life and doing all the things he wanted to do if he didn't have a full-time job. Dave is an avid operagoer and fan who likes to look for the funny side in anything. Opera gives him lots to look at. This book represents his sixth illustrative collaboration with David Barber.

Tenors, Tantrums and Trills
An Opera Dictionary from Aida to Zzzz

Published in Canada by

SOUND AND VISION
359 Riverdale Avenue
Toronto, Canada M4J 1A4

First printing, August 1996
1 3 5 7 9 11 13 15 - printings - 14 12 10 8 6 4 2

Canadian Cataloguing in Publication Data

Barber, David W. (David William), 1958-
Tenors, tantrums and trills

ISBN 0-920151-19-1

1. Opera - Dictionaries. 2. Opera - Humor
1. Donald, David C. 11. Title
ML102.06B3 1996 782.1'03 C96-931240-7

Typeset in Century Expanded

Printed and bound in Canada

Bach, Beethoven and the Boys
Music History as It Ought to Be Taught

Here's a book that chronicles the lives of the great (and not-so-great) composers as you've never read them before — exploring their sex lives, exposing their foibles and expanding our understanding of these remarkable but also all-too-human creatures. Chock-full of information, interesting facts and trivia, this hilarious history covers music from Gregorian chant to the mess we're in now. From Bach's laundry lists to Beethoven's bowel problems, from Gesualdo's kinky fetishes to Cage's mushroom madness, David Barber tells tales out of school that ought to be put back there. (Think how much more fun it would be if they taught this stuff.)

Now in a special new edition to celebrate the 10th anniversary of its first printing, *Bach, Beethoven and the Boys* has been updated and completely redesigned to better feature the wonderfully clever cartoon illustrations of Dave Donald.

You'll laugh, you'll learn, you'll love this book that writer Anthony Burgess has praised as being funnier than the classic *1066 And All That*.

ISBN 0-920151-10-8

Other Sound And Vision books by David W. Barber,
illustrated by Dave Donald:

A Musician's Dictionary

An irreverent and witty lexicon of musical terms, this collection of light-hearted and satirical definitions will delight musicians, non-musicians — and even singers.

ISBN 0-920151-03-5

When the Fat Lady Sings

Opera History as It Ought to Be Taught

From its humblest beginnings to its most overblown excesses, the story of opera is full of amazing facts and amusing fun. David Barber looks at the extravagant world of opera as only he can, with clever insight and puckish good humor.

ISBN 0-920151-11-6

If It Ain't Baroque

More Music History as It Ought to Be Taught

Having lambasted classical music's big-name composers, David Barber turns his trenchant wit to exploring its major genres. Symphonies, concertos, masses, Requiems, chamber music and more — all of the important forms composers have used through the ages come under scrutiny in this wickedly entertaining musical and historical guide.

ISBN 0-920151-15-9

Getting a Handel on Messiah

Handel's famous oratorio has become a beloved tradition for performers and audiences around the world, a musical statement of profound spiritual belief. But did you know that the first *Messiah* was rehearsed in a pub and performed in a theatre? Or that Handel stole some of the music from some of his own earlier saucy operatic arias? Learn all this and more in this waggish look at a familiar favorite.

ISBN 0-920151-17-5

Other music books from Sound And Vision:

Music Lover's Quotations
A Lyrical Companion
by Kathleen Kimball Melonakos
ISBN 0-920151-14-0

I Wanna Be Sedated
Pop Music in the Seventies
by Phil Dellio and Scott Woods
ISBN 0-920151-16-7

Love Lives of the Great Composers
from Gesualdo to Wagner
by Basil Howitt
ISBN 0-920151-18-3

How To Stay Awake
During Anybody's Second Movement
by David E. Walden
ISBN 0-920151-20-5

If you have any comments
on this book or any other books
that we publish, please write to us at
Sound And Vision, 359 Riverdale Avenue
Toronto, Ontario M4J 1A4, Canada
or Email us at
musicbooks@soundandvision.com